MIRIAM WADDINGTON

THE LAST LANDSCAPE

Toronto OXFORD UNIVERSITY PRESS 1992

Oxford University Press
70 Wynford Drive, Don Mills, Ontario M3C 1J9

Toronto   Oxford   New York
Delhi   Bombay   Calcutta   Madras   Karachi   Kuala Lumpur
Singapore   Hong Kong   Tokyo   Nairobi   Dar es Salaam
Cape Town   Melbourne   Auckland

and associated companies in
Berlin   Ibadan

This book is printed on permanent (acid free) paper.

Canadian Cataloguing in Publication Data

Waddington, Miriam, 1917—
        The last landscape

Poems.
ISBN 0-19-540904-3

I. Title.
PS8545.A32L37 1992   C811'.54   C92-093783-7
PR9199.3.W3L37 1992

OXFORD is a trademark of Oxford University Press
1 2 3 4 - 95 94 93 92
Printed in Canada by Hignell Printing Ltd.

Acknowledgements

Some of these poems were first published in the following periodicals: *Arc, Border Crossings, Canadian Forum, Canadian Journal of Women's Studies, CV II, Poetry Toronto, Quarry, Queen's Quarterly, The Structurist, Toronto Life.* I would like to thank Phyllis Wilson for her help with the manuscript.

Contents

For my friend Richard Teleky

THE SNOW TRAMP

When it snowed
in Winnipeg
my mother would look
out the kitchen window
and say
I wish I was a gypsy.

She would put on
her moccasins and
sweaters, wrap a scarf
around her neck, shoulder
her snowshoes and go
tramping
in Kildonan park.

That evening when
my father came home
he found us all supperless,
he was angry and worried
but he opened a can of soup
and fed us.

When my mother
came home it was late
and dark; she shook
the snow from her hair
and wondered how it happened
we didn't know she had gone
tramping
in Kildonan park.

My father scolded,
but my mother's soul

1

was far away
wrapped like a gift
in stars and snow,
and all night long
her gypsy tunes sang
and danced in the wind
around our house.

THE WOMAN IN THE HALL

1

There is a woman
in the hall,
she lives alone in
some upstairs room
in a nebulous city,
surely you have passed her
on your way to the bathroom;
and haven't you met her
coming out of the
communal kitchen?

Is she birdwoman or
sibyl, farmwife or
fishgutter, or is she
the buttonhole maker
who worked on the suit
you wear or maybe she's
the pastry decorator
who picks out the words
on the cakes you order?

Whoever she is
she is also Guernica
and Madrid she is Moscow
besieged and Dieppe
betrayed, she is all the
sombre-eyed girls in Goya's
drawings forever mourning
their soldier lovers forever
wandering through littered
battlefields forever
gathering fragmented faces

and gnawed-off limbs of
seventeen-year-old recruits.

2

That woman in the hall
is hunger and desolation,
she is the addled brain
of the crazy woman who
survived the camps to
to sit out her days on the
shores of the Dead Sea
muttering curses and
incantations, the woman
in the hall hears the
messages from beggars
in Berlin from street girls
in Buenos Aires.

3

In her sleep
the woman in the hall
sometimes sings lullabies,
her hair fans out on the
pillow in streams of
water and babies, her many
faces are covered with rain
and falling leaves her ears
tremble with whispers of
lost children but she knows
concealed in the white thigh
of every woman is a mouth,
the mother of all speaking.

4

Who is this woman
who dreams against guns
and hunger whose words
turn into songs as they
climb into higher and
higher skies? Is she
birdwoman or sibyl,
is she fishgutter or
buttonhole maker or is she
the quilter in some small
town eking out life on
a pension? Whoever she is
she hears your messages,

5

And turns the tides
with your anger and sorrow,
her wrists throb with the
pulse of ruined cities,
she dreams your dreams,
and scatters her muffled
words into your sleep;
she is the ragpicker who
comes to warn you
of future Guernicas,
and she is the woman who
at last awakens in you
your broken promises your
ancient righteousness.

INSTEAD OF LOVERS

I think I have
forgotten
how to love a man.

Long ago
in my youth
I loved many men,
touched them
with the red feathers
of my heart,
glided over them
with the yellow silk
of my hands
and sounded in them
the bells of my voice.

I embraced them
with the forest
of my arms
rocked them to sleep
on the clouds
of my breast and praised
their every awakening
with the whiteness
of morning.

Now I wonder
who plucked the feathers
of my heart,
who trampled the silk
of my hands,
who broke the bells,
chain-sawed the forest
and darkened

the whiteness of morning?
Are these the men
I loved?

As they draw nearer
I see
instead of lovers
a crowd of old men
coming to meet me,
they are dressed
in narrow suits of
carrion-crow black
they are making speeches
and shouting,
they are hoarse from
exhorting us
with their cracked old
promises of doves
and freedom.

They don't know
they are talking to the
deaf winds
in the space of yesterday,
to the blind snow
in the crevices
of aeons ago—
and as they walk
towards me each one
carries in his mouth,
like a dog his meat,
the body of a dead child.

This is the gift
they offer
to the women who bore them:

dead children.
Dead children
are the garland
they bring
to place on the grave
of the future.

FUTURES

After the spring and summer
of being twenty,
and the long sunny autumn
of being thirty,
we are suddenly in the winter
of being forty.

Being fifty
will be even deeper winter,
as for sixty—
it simply stands there waiting
for the weatherless season
of becoming seventy.

After that there is only
the frowzy worn-out path
to death,
or else the unlikely nudge,
the plunging shock
to a new awakening.

REFLECTIONS

How we photographed
ourselves
and each other when
we were young;

Now we avoid mirrors
and turn away
from reflecting
windows;

And these days
when we travel
we turn out the lights
lock up the house,

And leave our cameras
closed and shuttered,
safe in the darkness
of home.

THE LIFE OF A WOMAN

The life of a woman
is never in tune
with the times,
she is born too early
or too late and suffers
discords, interruptions,
humiliations and
surprise endings.

With the life of a woman
it's like with those
green bananas I buy
in the supermarket in winter,
they never seem to ripen
or grow sweet,
instead they turn black,
then they wither and shrink,
reminding me of a certain
raw and passionate love
that darkened my youth;

The one that never ripened
or grew sweet,
but withered into a death
emptier and colder
than the freezing corridors
of subway stations
after midnight.

KNIVES AND PLOUGHSHARES

The knife
is not a ploughshare
but a versatile instrument,
use it on your friends;
it works,
send it to your enemies,
they'll sharpen it,
give it to your mercenaries
as a matter of course,
or take it
to a dark street and plunge it
into a passing jogger,
it says nothing
political.

Better still
conduct an opera with it,
dance a Carmen
with the knife sharp
between your teeth
like a rose;
the knife—
flower of our
civilization.

THE ANGELS WHO SWEEP I

1

The angels
with the red lanterns
and frost-veined wings
are sweeping the night
from the snow cities,
they are sweeping drifts
from the forest paths,
they swing their lanterns
over the tops
of sleeping mountains.

Like picture angels
they almost fly.

2

Other messengers
with suffering eyes
and shaved heads
come from the moths,
from the dry nests
beyond the borders
of dark snow cities.
They sit in libraries
pretending to read,
their tongues are tied
and heavy with cold,
their heads on thin stems
flutter and nod,
their faces shrivel
to powdery dust,
they have no names.

Like old fences
they almost fall.

3

In my backyard
two lions prowl,
they have stepped down
from museum posters
of bright Jerusalem,
in my workroom
the dolls desert
their clever houses
and the pretty girls
who used to smile
from the tops of old
chocolate boxes
blacken their lips
and comb the mice
out of their hair;
they don't shop for
groceries anymore,
on Fridays they have
nowhere to go.

Like friends who turn,
they almost walk away.

4

The cruel stepmother
brassy and empty-breasted
meets with her cabinet,
she briefs the weather,
summons the winds
calls up the floods and

hastens the hurricanes;
at night she talks to us
on television; she smiles
into our living rooms,
while her secret army
chloroforms and gags us.

To the grinding of words
we almost sleep.

5

The white cats
go into the ravine,
the poplar trees
are bitten to the ground,
the sun hangs in the sky
like a naked bullet,
it scalds and deafens
the air.

6

The cherry tree flowers
and grows eyes,
its fruit is soft,
pale and big as apples,
the centre whitens
and withers.

The leaves stink
anger and helplessness.

7

A dove sits on a post
on the throughway,

a wispy flag
blows in the wind;
elsewhere perhaps
a green branch sleeps
in an old trunk
under the glacial shield.

The angels
with the red lanterns
continually sweep the snow
from the rivers and
they sweep the snow
from the glaciers,
they are tireless
in their sweeping,
but the watchmaker's clock
ticks and ticks
and knows no growing time,
no human season.

THE ANGELS WHO SWEEP II

1

The silence of angels:
their words are hushed
in the murmur of snow,
when they look up
from their sweeping
their brooms are frozen,
caught in the stillness
of winter's mid-air.

They incline their heads,
they are listening
to Beethoven play
his bursting song
when prisoners first see
the blinding light
through their barred
and buried windows.

2

The red lanterns of angels
hang waiting in mid-air
and the bells
in the golden throats
of church spires
ring between silences.

3

The blessed silence
of angels; like those
Sunday morning silences
when we walked through

city streets that were
half-asleep and empty,
and only the smells
of fresh bread and coffee
drifted down with us
to the river.

4

And the streets
in those days stretched
across shining bridges
to the unknown prairie
and the ripening future;
unmindful
we walked on the bridges
and admired the lacy
fretwork crocheted from
silvery steel by some
giant hand.

5

We did not ask
whose was the hand,
we did not read
the specific gravity
of girders or guess
at the composition,
the depth of the pilings.

6

Locked in our separate
trances, we joined
the invisible procession
towards what was still

undisclosed; and the angels
with the red lanterns
hovered over us,
their wings brushed us
with silence and the silence
was the silence
of the angels who sweep.

7

In our hearts we knew
it was not really summer.

LIVING WITH RUMOURS OF WAR

Cities close early
these days
wild people roam
the empty streets
the garbage cans are full
the furnaces are out,
the bus carrying people
to the suburbs never comes,
and there's a tall old man
around who keeps wondering
why he can't get a taxi.

THE LAST LANDSCAPE

I follow
the sky west
to another city,
drive through a ring
of cardinals, a wreath
of flowering birds;
the road dips
and I descend
to the dark lake.

There are
no sunsets here,
only men who beckon
through armoured windows
of plate glass;
their gray teeth shine
they offer me
porcelain words and
paper handkerchiefs
for my broken hands,
they give me documents
for safe-conduct
through the glass mountain
where some say many
are still imprisoned.

Below us sits
the queen of snow
on a soundless shore,
she is old and wrapped
in crusted shoals,
she strokes the sour waves
on her lap and mutters

doughty incantations;
in her oyster eyes
the milky seas rise
and fall.

I taste salt and
count the dead fish
on the beach; on the road
I drive past two clay bowls
and a startled cow,
I travel fast I stay
inside the white lines,
I don't want to scatter
the red petals
in the wreath of cardinals;
I don't want the birds
to fall out of the sky
in a rain of red flowers;

And most of all
I want to get past the rumour
of drowned countries
and no other cities,
I'm afraid—
I'm afraid I might touch
the hot grinding sound,
the cannibal roar
of the planet's death
when it begins to happen.

THE NEW JASONS

With the golden fleece
for cover
they pour our blood
into a bowl.

Then in some corridor
they find
a cracked basin
to catch
the magic rain
that falls
from the hat-brim
of that old hero
Jason.

These new Jasons,
their false words gilded,
steal
the golden fleece
and wrap
its shining folds
around their wild-rat
faces.

Then they fly
sated on flesh
of the young and
banqueted
on the sacs of our dead
futures.

With teeth bared
and stinking tongues,

they shriek
and fly into
the world's red night
of nevermore and terror
to do their murder:
war.

AMOS

Your justice was
a mere whisper
in the armed gardens
of Jerusalem.

In the noisy
sunshine your
justice glittered
and was subdued.

Your justice
shattered
on the broken
rocks of
Jerusalem,

And was enfolded
in the slashed
remnants
of its ancient
light.

ULYSSES EMBROIDERED

You've come
at last from
all your journeying
to the old blind woman
in the tower,
Ulysses.

After all adventurings
through seas and
mountains through
giant battles,
storms and death,
from pinnacles
to valleys;

Past sirens
naked on rocks
between Charybdis
and Scylla, from
dragons' teeth,
from sleep in
stables choking
on red flowers
walking through weeds
and through shipwreck.

And now you are
climbing the stairs,
taking shape,
a figure in shining
thread rising from
a golden shield:
a medallion

emblazoned in
tapestry you grew
from the blind hands
of Penelope.

Her tapestry
saw everything,
her stitches
embroidered the
painful colours
of her breath the
long sighing touch
of her hands.

She made many
journeys.

GARDENS AND US

Thirty years ago
full of plans and hopes
we moved into
brand new houses,
planted smoke-bush
and yew, mountain ash
and flowering crab,
painted and carpentered,
refinished old tables,
laid tile for patios,
scolded the children
and enrolled them
in junior hockey and
baseball clubs.

The children grew up
and moved away,
the yew grew to monster
size the crab attracted
tent caterpillars,
the quince scattered
its bitter fruit all over
the flower beds
with spiteful cunning,
the roses and wild
sweetpeas were rebellious,
rampant and out of control,
the black medoc, crabgrass,
and speedwell didn't care
what happened to the lawn,
and settled stubbornly
into cracks and crevices
in the driveway where

the earwigs and ants
daily multiplied.

The refinished tables
have lasted and still shine,
they preen themselves,
have become collectible
and sought after;
the painted walls
are pale and smooth,
bland and silent and
the chairs don't
talk to us.

But we have other
serious troubles—
the sour chemicals from
the golf course drift
across the valley
with the wind and kill
the phlox and even that
survivor, periwinkle, wilts;
the rabbits eat up
the parsley and marigolds,
but the garden is indifferent
and passive, has become old
and introverted, returns us
none of the old love
we lavished on it.

The butterflies are gone,
there are no more toads,
but the cardinals
still come, they sing
to us at suppertime,

otherwise the street
is quiet as the grave
and so are we as we take
our dutiful walks;
we are practicing to be
future ghosts of ourselves
who will return
in spring to haunt
the old neighbourhood.

PAPER BOATS

When we divorced,
we each divorced our youth,
sent it like paper boats
sailing to who knows where,
and lost our selves
in those old lovers' lanes
still winding
through our blood.

In my blood
the self has dwindled,
and the lovers' lanes
have faded,
but in your blood
our youth still dreams
and winds its way
through the remote rivers
of your death.

QUESTIONS

Why do I still dream
of lovers, hikes along
the Gatineau and
autumn bonfires beside
Fairy Lake?

Why do I think
of the cindery
canal paths beside
Ottawa's driveway the
rosy tulips of spring
and the leaves ankle-
deep in September?

And when walking
across Laurier Bridge
blind as a sleepwalker why
do I keep glimpsing
myself aged sixteen?

Aged sixteen: and why
do I keep seeing
the man who became
my husband walking
towards me

In a future
that lies so far
behind me?

LANGUAGES

Once a man came to my door
selling storm windows,
he asked me was I a widow
and the answer was yes.
I married him and he begged me
to teach him better English
so he could drive a taxi.

After some years
we went different ways,
I taught people
in many schools how
to speak better English
and I forgot the storm windows
and the man who sold them.

Until one day
jumping into a taxi
to go to one of my schools
to teach people how
to speak better English,
I gave the taxi driver
directions and he turned
around to me and said:

Do you remember storm windows
and how widowed you were?
I'm married again
I have a little boy
I speak good English
plain for everyday;

But your English,
it's pretty your English
is like a flower.

MECHANICS FOR WOMEN

Late in life
I am finding out
the immortal names
of screwdrivers.

First there is
the plain screwdriver,
then there is
the star-shaped one
called Phillips,
and a few in-between ones
whose names
I never learned.

There are also wrenches,
open and closed,
and hammers, soft-faced
or hard-lipped,
and pliers called
needle-nosed or blunt
like fish swimming
through the mighty
mechanical lakes
of the universe.

Among all the tools
I love the spanners
best because
you can do anything
with spanners
depending on the size
of them,
and you soon learn

which spanner to use
when and what signs
spell trouble in the
universal joint.

It's all so easy
so enchanting so
original, from
the newest sparkplug
to the smallest
distributor cap.
Oh the wonderful
the beautiful the
absorbing folklore
of tools!

Yet I still find it
impossible
to change a flat tire.

THE SUMMER GIRLS

Under the awnings
of street cafes striped
with runaway sunlight,
the summer girls
in their flowered dresses
are eating their lunches.

They have only an hour
but have dreamed
for a lifetime of the
far snowy mountains
and green-painted rivers
that run icy cold
over sand-bars and pebbles
that flicker and blind
them with glintings
of gold.

They see themselves
flying and hear
themselves landing on
spongy marsh grasses
among Indian paint pots
of vermilion and ochre,
colours that time
with its patience and
patchwork has coaxed
from the stone.

They see themselves
bending like trees
in the water their
faces refracting the
leap of the light,

they feel their hair
loosening luxurious
and falling on shoulders
of August,

Far from the corridors
and clocks of their
earnings, far from
the memos that nag
and harass them,
out of reach of the
telephone with its
hiccups and jangles
breaking into their
trances, their daydreams
and longings.

When the hour is over
they rise from the tables
and turn to leave
their oases of canvas
the striped awning cafes.
They float and they fly
across prairies and fences
to their downtown offices
where the wet mouth
of the city slobbers and
swallows them.

Yet somehow the colour
of the Indian paint pots
trails and follows them,
and the washed rags
of laughter clothe
and caress them
the whole afternoon.

IN THE HURLY BURLY ARCADE

When she was a child
she killed her mother
and married her father;
later as a young woman
she poisoned her lovers;
was it her fault they died?

Disillusioned with men
she entered a university
and gave herself to books;
gradually the books piled up
and grew tall against the
windows, they begot children
upon her, dwarfs and hunchbacks
and a single willowy girl
with skyblue eyes.

When she was middle-aged
her waist thickened and
her behind flattened from
sitting so much in libraries,
she began not to sleep well
and to have nightmares,
she dreamed the willowy one
was poisoning the sherry
or lurking on the balcony
among the disused summer
furniture or else
she was waiting to meet her
on the stairs so she could
push her headlong down.

One day she went downtown
secretly to buy a bus ticket
to Vancouver but when she
got to the bus station all
the good seats were taken;
most of the time she sat beside
bushy-haired seventeen-year-old
girls and their pale babies,
or else men in big black hats
who smelled under the armpits
squeezed in beside her.

The journey to the coast
took longer than she expected,
she bought a lot of sandwiches
in Winnipeg and they lasted
most of the way to Regina;
somewhere near Rogers Pass
they sold cheap coffee
then the bus went through
Crow's Nest Pass where the
farmers were still picketing
for lower freight rates.

Finally she got to Vancouver;
Gastown was bleak and empty
as a prairie railway stop
and she hadn't really had
any adventures so she decided
to take the ferry to Victoria
where she found Emily Carr's
boarding house was under new
management; all her friends

were dead or living in tidy
retirement homes.

What was she to do? The best thing
was to go back to her own city
and make guarded peace
with the willowy daughter.
She would work hard at becoming
invisible for the years
that remained to her; she would
haunt the libraries and read all
their books, she would take notes
and do a lot of xeroxing, she would
eat her lunches on benches downtown
or at McDonald's where they give
old women free coffee.

After all her travels
she would end up with this
small wisdom; how to find
warm places and free coffee.

KLARA AND LILO

What wind, you have to ask, had blown them to the Rancho Rio Cantara, these two freckled, brightly coloured old birds with their big busts and stomachs, dyed hair, and German accents? For that matter, what wind had blown me to the Rancho that winter? There must be hundreds of spas in Mexico, so why did I decide to spend my midwinter break at this one and no other? Especially as it's so hard to get to from Toronto. You have to fly to Dallas, change for Guadalajara, and then take a taxi that bumps you over twenty-five miles of cobblestone road into a national park famous for its high altitude and healing hot springs.

The Rancho took only fifty guests. Most of them were Yoga devotees, psychics, and spiritual healers with a few retired couples thrown in who came to bathe in the mineral springs. It was a little like a kibbutz in that we all had our own adobe huts, each with its own fireplace, yet we ate communally at long wooden tables in the dining room. Conversation at meal times, although not elevating, was at least not about the body, its health or diet, but mostly about new ways to get in touch with your unconscious. To this end the Rio Cantara offered Felsenkreis, Alexander method, Yoga and Acupuncture, and there were guests who would cast your horoscope, read your palm, or tell your fortune from the vibrations of your aura. There was also a weathered little woman from Seattle who played the guitar and sang old cowboy numbers like 'I'm Sending you a Big Bouquet of Roses' and 'Her Name was Lil and She was a Beauty and Lived in a House of Ill Repute-y'—songs I hadn't heard since my college days.

One Friday morning after Yoga class I was settling down to read in one of the lounge chairs around the

41

pool. I had just opened Anita Brookner's *Providence* when one of the freckled ladies who had arrived the day before sat down beside me. She wanted to talk. At first I wasn't too happy about it; I remembered the arrival of the two sisters—for such they turned out to be—and how they had looked like a couple of beat-up parrots with half their feathers missing and the other bedraggled half sticking out every which way under garish red and yellow sun-hats. The one now at my side was still wearing the sun-hat and a dressmaker bathing-suit from the nineteen-thirties. But her face, under her dyed red hair, was composed and all her feathers were back in place.

I resigned myself to not reading, shut my book, and listened. Klara had a low voice with gravel caught in its timbre, which emphasized her heavy Viennese accent. To this day I don't know why she chose me to sit beside, except that I look Jewish, but after that day Klara always sought me out at the poolside. Her sister Lilo was a swimmer, and spent most mornings doing lengths. Sometimes she stopped and chatted with us for a few minutes, but mostly she was in the pool.

Even now, four years later, when I close my eyes I see the pool and the steamy vapours rising from the river that flows through the ranch. And I hear the blur of murmuring sound from which Klara's voice always emerges with slow vibrancy and careful succinctness. She is talking, always talking. About what? First it's the past. Given the place and time they lived in, it's a life like other Jewish lives—in no way remarkable. In the thirties they were Jews living in Vienna, yes, but who thought about it? 'We weren't always old and dumpy like now', Klara smiles out of her very clear, very large green eyes. They're shallow as a wading pool with an opaque skin of calmness that doesn't let you really look into them.

Klara talks. Lilo is a book-keeper—'You should have seen her. So pretty, fair, with rosy cheeks and best of all she's afraid of no one.' She, Klara, the older sister, is a children's doctor. 'It wasn't easy even before the war, no, not even then. But when has it ever been easy?' But she persists and in 1938 she is working in a children's clinic in one of Vienna's poor sections. She laughs. 'I was an idealist. Not practical like Lilo, who when she reads in the paper that Jews aren't allowed to sit on park benches with Austrians, wastes no time, lines up outside the British Consulate and gets a visa to emigrate to England. As a maid. Some maid! A Jewish girl who can't even boil water, her head is so full of numbers. Only numbers interest her. It's still the same.'

But in those days everyone was working in factories in England, even the maids. Only immigrants were left to work in the rich houses—mostly German girls. Where was it she worked? Somewhere in the north, in a castle where everybody freezes and they don't give a maid enough to eat. 'And Lilo is writing me come, begging me, "Come, don't wait." But I don't want to leave. Just think, there are so many little children! I love my work and they are still keeping me in the clinic. My director is not so bad, not all the Austrians hate Jews. Things will get better, it has to be.

'But Lilo pesters me. She runs everywhere, to all the offices, she sends me papers. They come and three days later there is war, and I am a maid with Lilo in the same castle. We keep each other warm at night, we sleep in sweaters, I knit socks. Thursday is our day off and all us maids go to the village, we meet in a café, we have tea. The English—you know how tea is their life.'

And the rest of the story? Again ordinary. I've heard it all, read it all before, I don't know why I'm listening except that Klara makes it interesting. Maybe it's her voice, or the sun, or this out-of-the-way place. I hear how neither Klara nor Lilo marry, there's just no time. Lilo is busy going to night school, learning English. Soon she has a job, but Klara isn't so lucky. She has no talent for the language. 'Your verb to be—am, were, was, be, be—all those bees.' She can never learn it. And how can you be a doctor for children without English? Besides, she has no money. The best she can do is work as a technical assistant in a children's clinic in Leeds. 'About Leeds what can I say? The people, they're good, they're kind, they're nice, but after Vienna, who can live in Leeds?'

When the war is over the sisters get a letter from an uncle in Montreal. They write back and forth and the upshot is, he brings them over. 'You needed a sponsor and all kinds of papers, not like today.' But at least they're together. She and Lilo get an apartment on Van Horne near Victoria, in those days a nice Jewish district if you know Montreal. Lilo has no trouble—right away she starts to work for an accountant. But Klara is miserable. For her to learn English is like climbing the Alps. And friends in Vienna, those who are left, begin to write and urge her to come back. They need doctors in Vienna, even her old clinic that was bombed has been rebuilt.

But she hesitates. She feels ashamed that she wants to go back after what they did to the Jews, and she doesn't want to leave Lilo. But what kind of life can she have in Montreal? She misses her work. Children don't have prejudices, they don't know from anti-Semitism. When she decides to go back—in 1951, to be exact—Lilo agrees just so long as they can meet twice a year for three weeks in winter and again in summer.

Klara stops talking. I open my eyes and she smiles at me. I smile back. One thing I notice. Although Klara talks freely and enjoys it, she always becomes vague when I ask her the details about how she got back to Vienna. And I don't probe—I've met enough refugees to know that you don't ask. You listen.

She does say something that stays in my mind. 'You know, to survive is not always the most important thing, I didn't want to live my life only or mostly as a survivor, to have the idea to save my life always uppermost. What kind of a life could I have in Leeds, in Montreal? I was an outsider, I didn't fit in, I was not at home. What is a person without a life's work, if there is no purpose except to stay alive? I wanted to breathe the air I grew up in, no matter how everything changed. I knew that the earth, the air, the forests of my childhood would always be the same, would always know my footsteps when I returned.

'And I wanted to feel useful, to heal children, to talk to their mothers in the only language I knew. I said to myself, "Klara, there are more important things than survival. To survive and live half-dead is no kind of life."' She sighs and ends with one of those remarks older people like to make to younger ones. 'Yes, in life you pay for everything.'

Then these serious matters are lost, in a welter of appealing trivialities. Such as the matter of Klara's man-friend. He's a bachelor. Like herself, he never married. They have dinner together every day except for the six weeks she spends with Lilo. How long have they been together? Without blinking an eyelash she tells me: 'Thirty-three years.' It works very well—they each have their own apartment, their own bank account, their own tastes. Of course he misses her while she's with Lilo, but she needs that time, not only because of Lilo, but to refresh herself. For example, up to this year she and Lilo have always gone to the Canaries in winter. Klara gives me a precise description of the wonderful little hotel they patronize there. I take out my notebook and write down the name of the hotel and the proprietor and all the details. She is even more enthusiastic about their summer getaway in the mountains, and her eyes light up as she tells me about Merano in the Italian Dolomites. I've never heard of it, but I listen to a description of the Hotel Peterhof, its location, the names of the proprietors, and the way they had it decorated with everything handmade, handcarved, and handwoven. I can see the fresh white linen curtains with their embroidered borders, the breakfast room with its blue earthenware cups, the lime tree outside the back windows, and the road that runs in front of the hotel separating it from a spring-fed mountain lake. I had never known anyone who had been to the Dolomites, but there and then I made up my mind to spend my next European holiday near Merano at Klara's Hotel Peterhof.

So the week passed. We did Yoga every morning and joined the group hike to explore the surrounding country. Afterwards people bathed naked in the walled pool set aside for that purpose, or sat under umbrellas by the main pool. In the afternoons some guests went for a walk. The next village was two kilometres away over rough cobblestones—fine if you had good shoes with thick soles, but there was an easier walk if you followed the river that ran through the Rancho for about half a mile to a waterfall.

One afternoon Klara and I decide to walk there. The path is sandy and narrow and we have to walk single file. The sand is so fine and white that it's hard to plough through it with our shoes on. So we take them off and walk barefoot, scuffing our feet through the warm sand.

The walk takes longer than we think and the landscape

doesn't appeal to my Canadian eyes. It's all stunted and
gnarled trees, craggy rocks, and wide-hipped hills that
sprawl sloppily against a woundingly hot sky. The sun
beats down on us, so we're glad when we reach the
waterfall. We leave our shoes on the bank, take off our
T-shirts, and pick our way carefully over a series of flat
rocks to where the water slips over the ledge and
cascades down in a shower. We sit and let the water
splash over us, enjoying its warmth and telling each
other how healthy it is, with our skins absorbing all those
good minerals. We talk about the winter we're missing,
with its dark nights and rain. It is utterly quiet except
for an occasional bird and the sound of water, which
soothes us until we're almost nodding. But we don't let
ourselves fall asleep; instead we get up and climb up the
bank to the opposite side so we can take a different way
home. Klara needs a hand to get up the bank—she's
seventy, after all—and we start back. Our feet are still
wet and the sand on this side of the river is damp too.
This is the shady side. Klara walks ahead of me. My feet
are big and make deep marks in the sand. I see with
satisfaction that at least my feet aren't flat; the arch
doesn't sink into the sand but forms a crescent in each
footprint.

I glance ahead to see how Klara's feet are doing. I read
somewhere that old people's feet are nearly always flat
and I want to know if that's true. I see Klara walking a
few yards ahead, but realize with a start that she isn't
leaving any footprints in the sand. None at all! At first
I'm puzzled. Then I'm sort of scared. How can it be? I
can't really let myself believe it. Should I say something?
Should I ask her? No, it's better to just keep walking,
pretend I haven't noticed.

I try to rationalize. I tell myself maybe it's because
she's so small. Small yes, but not exactly light; and

certainly not light enough. Maybe there are no foot-
prints because the sand is dry up ahead where she's
walking. When I get there I see it isn't dry; it's the same
sand that sucks at my feet and makes me sink heavily
into it.

I begin to wonder if there isn't something odd about
Klara. I don't believe in all that psychic stuff about auras
and reincarnation that's floating around at the spa. At
the same time Klara's clothes are terribly old-fashioned.
And what about her hair? Dyes are a lot better these days
than what Klara's using. And Klara did something few
other Jews have done. She went back to Vienna and
turned her back on America. She said some odd things
too. 'To survive is not all-important'—that isn't a Jewish
thought. She also said it's better to be dead than half
dead. A lot of Jews would find that idea disloyal, as if
she were dismissing everything that survivors lived
through and suffered. And to go back to Vienna? It's all
very well to lose yourself in work, to find a purpose in
life through your work, but who do you talk to at night,
after work? Who do you go to the movies with, or how
exchange recipes? Of course I know the answer to
that—Klara has a man friend. I wonder if he knows she
doesn't leave footprints? And if he knows, does he care?
I'm not even sure that I care. I just can't help wondering.

When it comes time for the sisters to leave, Klara gives
me her address. 'You must come to visit me next time
you're in Europe,' she urges. 'Come to Vienna and stay
with me. I have an extra room for when Lilo comes.'
And she carefully writes out her address and phone
number. I give her my Toronto address too—I would
enjoy seeing her again. I like her exactness, her preci-
sion, the pragmatism, the lack of sadness.

I tell her not to expect me in Vienna, but I promise
to go to Merano, to the Hotel Peterhof. We say all these

things as Klara and Lilo are getting into the taxi. They are wearing their red and yellow sun-hats, and as the taxi lurches out of the Rancho they open the window and wave.

A year later I went to Merano and looked for the Hotel Peterhof at the address Klara had given me. There was no Hotel Peterhof. There had been one long ago before the war, but it had been used by German soldiers during the occupation and on its site now stood a row of high-rise condominiums.

As for Klara and Lilo themselves: I wrote to Dr Klara in Vienna but my letter was returned. When I made further inquiries I learned that she had never left Austria, had never joined Lilo, but died in a concentration camp in 1942. As for Lilo, her apartment house in Montreal was real enough, but she was no longer there. Neighbours told me that she had drowned years ago in a lake in the Laurentians where she had a cottage.

I still think about Klara walking ahead of me in the sand, leaving no footprints. I can't seem to get her out of my mind, and when I close my eyes she's always there: 'Look, we were not always so old and dumpy,' and 'Lilo had such rosy cheeks and was afraid of no one,' and 'To survive is not always the only thing or the best thing.' I keep telling myself that the wind that blew those two into the Rancho Rio Cantara that day in February must be the same wind that has now spirited them away, complete with sun-hats and flowered dresses, to a place where Klara heals little children in a clinic that never closes, while Lilo, the champion swimmer, swims end-less lengths in a sunlit pool where the summer never ends.

49

MOUNTAIN INTERVAL I: STUDIO

We look
through the window
see tree branches
nibbles of grass
and traces of elk where
the antlers were rubbed;
we sniff
chipmunk and squirrel
follow
barrel shadows
of bear.

Then undergrowth
shoots
arrows of sun
into chrome yellow
light,
we track footprints
and fossils
in secrets of stone.

We wait;
in that silence
hear
trees fall, see
ghosts walk,
they look over
their shoulders then
turn and beckon us
up to the heights,
to the slide
of the glaciers.

We dissolve
into nothingness
but our old antlered
hope rubs off
on the tree trunks
and grows in the grasses
for children to scatter
in the seeds of their
laughter
a hundred years later;

Or until the last
silence
descends on
these mountains and
fills up the distance
with waterfalls
falling.

MOUNTAIN INTERVAL II:
POW WOW AT BRAGG CREEK

I compose
grasses
turn words
on a loom
thread the yellow
of sun through needles
of sharp
mountain moonlight

2

I sing the flow
of golden streams
over ochre pathways
the fingers
of gravity in
the infinite pools,
the yielding of
marsh grass
to the forces
of water

3

I sing the snowy
smile of mountains
over hazy plains
over sweetgrass meadows
that sleep like
children under
skies and rains

4

My sleep is
dreamless
bound with belts
and crossed with
beads,
swift coyote tails
fly past with
the wind

5

I am dizzied
by bird faces
owl masks and eagles
in endless procession
I am deafened by
drumbeats blinded
by dust
and the swoop of
the dancers

6

They circle
and move
in their shining
numbers in their
myriad thousands,
thundering ravens

7

Dust rises
and falls

its clouds cloak
the dancers
until tireless
they ride
away into distance

8
They disappear
and are lost
on the shimmering
roads

PLACES

In that country
we heard distant moon music
and cuckoo cries,
in those days we filled
our baskets with beads
and coloured Sundays,
but in this country
there are only handbills
junk mail and free coupons,
they pile up in our mailboxes
and no one has time
to read them.

Instead we wait
for love-letters from
South America,
we speak words heavy
with corncob wisdom
and sometimes we wonder
what is so wonderful
about longevity when
so many are dying young,
some from hunger, others
from war, disease, and poisoned
waters while still others
just hang themselves.

Who is left to speak
for those who are dying?
Silently the artists
enter their workrooms,
slowly they carve out
nests and flowers inside

themselves in the long
darkness; outside there is
noise of civil war and
the fading summer.

On a distant hilltop
in the stone tower
of a capital city
carillon bells are ringing
their songs; homeless children,
surplus grain and rumours
of barricades, bayonets, and
broken bridges.
The rivers listen and grieve,
the hills hear and mourn;
as for ourselves we are
packing for a journey.

We fold our sober snows
and winter wisdom into
big trunks and ship them off
on pirate tankers to places
with tropical names where
black pepper grows under
the glossy leaves of never–
never–Monday morning trees.
Years from now
we will tell ourselves stories
about those imagined countries,
places where to this day
no one ever dances and
no one ever sings.

A FEW THINGS

There are only a few things
the politicians of war
or the privateers of
free enterprise
haven't yet found out
how to do.

These are to have dreams
and raise children,
be kind and human,
let birds nest
and trees and rivers
live.

ASPECTS OF OWLS I

1

Certain owls are golden
you can see them
sometimes
asleep at the bottom
of very deep wells

It is comforting
the way they wait
for a pebble to fall
through the many
transparencies
that tremble
the countless arches
that rise
always in water

2

Owls wait
for the pebble to fall
into the absolute region
at the brink
of their stillness

3

It is startling
to watch the single
zigzag shiver
of motion
that both announces
and delivers
its own birth

from the golden point
in an owl's golden
eye

4

The golden eye
flickers
at the bottom
of every deep well

ASPECTS OF OWLS II

1

It is necessary
to respect owls
they are aspects
of future
odd little fragments
of feeling

2

They are
drowsy messengers
they send us downy
letters and soft words
they whisper
of our lost seasons

They write us
about the white weather
of the nineteen-thirties
sealed now
under canals heavy
with plutonium

They write us
about twentieth-century
skating rinks
flooding the fields
with vapour

Also about deserts
of frozen ash
heaving
with the blind cries
of the unborn

3

Under the feathers
of this new darkness
the unborn lie
and the owls sleep
their uneasy days
wrapped in our own
endangered sleep

4

Somewhere perhaps
muffled rumours
and faint traces
of the golden eye
flicker
in the bottom of
an old well.

FREEDOM GAMES

The stars unbutton
their tight jackets
they peel off
their silver shirts
and naked dive
from cloudy springboards
into widening pools
of night.

And we below
are fishes lost
in the murky deeps,
blindly
we swim our way
through caves and tunnels
of unstable water
to the wavering light.

And always
we strive to surface,
and always
we stretch and strain
to force
our fishy bodies upwards
in a leap
towards the height.

And as we leap
all of us
are silvered by
showering meteors and
shreds of shining stuff;
frisky in our play

we dart and turn
until we are discovered
by your telescopes.

You chart
and label us
and carefully engrave
our Latin names
on little metal plates
that spell captivity.
And so you put an end
to fishy somersaults
and all our freedom games.

Then you enclose us
in watery boxes,
and sluice us through
the gates that keep us
prisoner
in the stone museums
of your dying states.

A MAN AND HIS FLUTE

A man in a black coat
plays a song
on a black flute
in a concert hall.
He plays with his whole
body with his hands
with his trunk until
he becomes a tree and
his arm a branch;
his fingers are urgent
extensions that startle
the air in the leaves.

His song is obscurely
about a lemon
picked from an old tree
in another country then
brought home and cut
against the blue
of a winter sky.

The lemon and the
black flute and the man
in the black coat who
sways with the music
in the concert hall
takes the blue sky the
yellow lemon and the
cold sunlight of March
and turns it into an April
filled with the blueness
of hyacinth; winter turns
its back and melts away

in the runnelled snow piled
against frozen houses.

The man and his flute
play their song,
the audience is pierced
by the blueness of sky,
the audience hears
the snow melting,
the audience sees spring
approaching the audience
stands up the audience claps,
the audience dances.

The man and his flute
end their song,
a smell of cut lemon
fills the air.

ORCHESTRA

Let me sing myself
into the very centre,
the sunheart
of a flower.
And sing myself
out again on the
high-low scales
of wind
its majors and
minors.

Then sing myself
away on all those
transparent
enchantments of climate
where a thousand bees
are humming
under the baton
of a single hand.

AUTUMN

(for Lyubomir Levchev)

When shall we visit
the garden of our friends
again?
When shall we again
break the walnuts
of September
and leaf through books
and argue again
about literature?

And when
in what year will we
again eat grapes
from the vineyard
of the poet's father
or drink the wine
of three harvests ago?

SCIENCE AND LITERATURE

The scientist sits and worries
about very ultimate problems:
take the permeability
of the cell wall—
how does protoplasm move
through the cell wall anyway
and how does it know when
to start or where to stop?
That's one problem,
and if we knew the answer
to that we'd have
the cure for cancer for
radiation burns and even
for old age—maybe.

Another ultimate problem:
take the curvature of space
and how to measure it;
imagine a doughnut the
scientist says all the surfaces
are curved and now imagine
a ladybug trying to crawl
over that same doughnut,
you mean how are you going
to figure out those distances
I ask intelligently or is it
simply a matter of $X+Y=Z$?
After all I say defensively
I studied high school calculus
trigonometry and algebra
such as they were of course
in the olden days.

And I add: wasn't James Joyce
doing the same thing in different
terms when he claimed language,
mere words, could change the way
blood flowed and hormones worked?
No no the scientist says
that's not it at all it's a matter
of dimension what you have to do
is grasp the fourth dimension!
(*go and catch a falling star*).

Well I say that's really hard
you're right X+Y=Z is just
child's play compared to
curvature; I think James Joyce
must have skipped that fourth
dimension and gone straight on
to the fifth without doing
the proper calculations but
you being a scientist, you still
have to worry about ladybugs
crawling on doughnuts and
measuring distance on the
curvature of space and
I suppose many even more
ultimate problems.

THE WRITER

Wanting to write the stories of ordinary Canadians I discover there are no ordinary Canadians. Of course you can always pick out Canadians in foreign airports by the red and white Air Canada tickets they're holding in their hands, and you can sometimes recognize them in the railway stations of European cities by the little gold maple leaf pins they wear in their lapels; they are anxious not to be mistaken for Americans. For some reason they consider themselves purer or more honest; anyway, different.

I wake up at 3 A.M. wanting to write stories about representative Canadians. And I wonder who else wakes up at 3 A.M.? For starters let's say it's women unrequitedly in love with Marcel or Harold. Marcel and Harold are really the same person, it's just that one disguises himself as the other at certain times. One stays in Toronto while the other travels the planes between Halifax and Vancouver looking for victims. They are probably a little bit malicious—Marcel and Harold—for they know that by dividing themselves like this they will be sure not to miss any of the women who are going to fall unrequitedly in love with them. One other thing. Marcel and Harold need all this unrequited love. It gives them a sense of well-being. Unless other people around them are suffering they can't be sure that they are not. This way they feel alive, the other way they would feel like dead mushrooms on an Algonquin trail, or discarded beer cans on the top of Mount Royal, or maybe two dead fish littering the beach at Spanish Banks in Vancouver. They might even become surrealistic figures in somebody's dream, these two phantom lovers. But this way, with people waking up at 3 A.M. to love them unrequitedly, they can achieve existence. They can be real.

Other people who wake up in the middle of the night are single women from Toronto living their August vacations in cooperatively rented cottages on Georgian Bay. They wake up when they hear the mice scraping against the rafters under the roof. They suddenly feel scared and turn the lights on, take a drink of water from the glass on the night table and remind themselves to wash out their white blouses and underwear in the morning. Then they swallow two aspirins and if they still can't get to sleep after all that, they fall into easy fantasies whose details are dim but whose personnel is drawn from among the mechanics at the Volvo garage where they get their 3000 mile check-ups.

I'm the one who wakes up to the whine and buzz of mosquitoes who somehow got through the screen. I wonder why I haven't got an ulcer or a weak heart or arthritis yet. I decide to open a coffee house on Grand Manan and learn to play the guitar. I face the empty space in my double bed and remember the nightmare of driving on expressways. Then I turn on the light and tell myself that tomorrow is another day. I have things to do. The wind to listen to, the sun to sit in, a leaf to pick and representative Canadians to write the stories of before everything starts all over again and turns out who knows how?

SPRING NIGHT AT HOME

I'm home tonight
with the chickens and goats,
there is no car in my carport
just darkness and the wind.

Beyond the darkness
the garden shivers with cold,
leftover frost is still hanging around
although it's spring;
look how the daffodils
are freezing, swollen with cold,
beaten down and battered,
(but their feet are warm
wrapped in the bulby bedsocks
of earth).

Can anyone tell me
why the trees look blind
and shake from their canes
and their branches bunches
of curly newborn leaves
while the forsythia bush
in the northeast corner blazes
with yellow lamps vulgarly
advertising spring?

The japonica on the west side
is more modest, lies there
snug and small in its place
in the gardenbed and lowers
its red flower-nipples
to suckle the earth and
all the time the hawthorn tree

is busy shining its blossoms
like searchlights
into the naked night.

Isn't it strange
how on this night the trees
float like moon islands
through the valley,
and how across the highway
two frogs are singing
and losing themselves
in the hum of traffic?

And here I am home tonight
with the chickens and goats,
they're all asleep—
and I'm waiting for morning
so the sun can come in
and help me to feed the world.

JACQUES CARTIER IN TORONTO

Do we ever think about Jacques Cartier
as we pilot our cars downtown
through a river of streets
looking for safe new harbours?
And do we ever think of green fields
or cows as we make our way later
through the vast acreages
of office and department store?

And do we feel the drought
on miles of western townships
as we water our city lawns
with green plastic sprinklers?
We read that the reservoirs
are empty that the corn is dying,
that even the marshes and wetlands
have dried into colourless chaff.

We shrug and go into our houses,
(the world was always hungry
and now it is thirsty too),
we shower and change we are ready
to board our cars and pilot them
across the city to distant restaurants,
our weekend gateways to Cathay.

Do we ever remember
that somewhere above the sky
in some child's dream perhaps
Jacques Cartier is still sailing,
always on his way always
about to discover a new Canada?

JACQUES CARTIER IN WINNIPEG

We never dreamed about you
Jacques Cartier,
Russia was very far
from your Saint Malo;
there were no telegrams
of congratulation from us
when you sailed down
the broad Saint Lawrence,
and you never entered
the minds of Winnipeg's
immigrant children.

So what was our life
those days on the prairie?
It was mornings
in fields of blue vetch
and on road-banks of clover,
it was games before dark,
Hiding-O-Seek and
Red Rover Red Rover.

Those ghostly children
still hold hands in a circle,
they turn and dance,
as their thin high voices
fall through the clouds
in a chorus of chanting:
Red Rover Red Rover we call
Jacques Cartier over!

You hear them and smile
and you come running over.

THE BOUQUET

She goes to answer the door. A man with a round face in a cap with loose earflaps hands her a basket of flowers done up in a transparent plastic bag. She can see they are flowers rare in winter: pink and mauve roses, freesias, irises, tall lemony snapdragons. And many thickleaved opaque green ferns wired and stuck in among strawflowers dyed different shades of purple. She has hated purple ever since as a child she had a bedroom painted mauve with a thin purple line where the ceiling met the wall. It was a sad lonely colour, a scarlet-fever, diphtheria-sort-of-colour, a disease-of-childhood colour, a castor-oil-floating-in-patches-on-a-glass-of-orange juice colour. The special children's doctor told her mother to put castor oil in the orange juice and her mother always followed his instructions to the letter.

Her mother loved the old Scottish doctor with his white hair and thick silver moustache and heavy burr and the way he came all the way across the city from his office in the children's hospital whenever she called him on a cold winter morning. He liked it that she always followed his instructions to the letter. Give them apple-sauce nothing better for children than applesauce and a dose of castor oil in orange juice. Nothing better. And her mother always followed his instructions to the letter.

She goes to the door. She remembers she thought yellow a good colour for walls and ceilings. Later when she had her own house she painted the kitchen walls yellow. Yellow, a heavy buzzing zig-zaggy colour like a migraine headache.

She takes the bouquet from the man with the loose earflaps and signs for it. Who sent it? She cannot imagine. She is old and no longer has suitors. Most of them are dead or close to it.

Maybe she should have stayed with purple. Unlike her mother she has never known a Scottish doctor with a silver moustache who would always come when she called him all the way across the city on a cold winter morning. All her life there was no one. No one who would give instructions which she could follow to the letter.

She searches the bouquet for a card. The roses and snapdragons smell of hothouse and wet earth. Who sends her flowers? There will be something written somewhere on a card. It will give instructions about how to care for the flowers. She knows she will follow them to the letter.

REMEMBERING WINNIPEG

How are you Winnipeg
of the wide streets
and colonnaded art school
near the train station?
How are you old city
with your broken accents
Ukrainian farmers and
Jewish welders? I miss you
city of small tailors,
cheap stores, back lanes,
and houses with glassed-in
verandas.

How is your black earth
below the frost line,
and how are those ghosts
of buffalo herds and hunters,
I wonder if you still hear
the big horses ploughing
and are they still riding
over the prairies in cabriolets
with bells ringing
and red fringes flying?

I hear that your skies
have turned cannibal,
that your rivers are slimy
and your ghosts now wander
through ragged lanes
fighting with broken bottles
in the glittering midnight;
Winnipeg, your house is on fire,

on fire, and your children
are burning!

So summon your winds
from all the four corners
to fly with the news
that a storm is brewing,
and clean rain is coming
on clouds from the north
to clear all the pathways
of shadows and debris,
to make room for the light.

So I can say hello Winnipeg,
hello to your wide streets
and narrow rivers,
hello to your summer boulevards
and lazy cemeteries,
greetings and *l'chaim* to your
Siberian caragana hedges.

And good luck
to all the freight cars
sleeping in your railway yards,
good luck to the abattoirs
of St. Boniface, to its golden
crosses and fearsome statues,
bonne chance to Louis Riel
wherever he is and a last salute
to the haunted house on the edge
of old Fort Garry.

Shake hands Winnipeg
remember me in the evenings

when the mosquitoes hum,
think of me at noon
when the cabbage butterflies
hover; don't forget me, Winnipeg,
when the frost strums its banjo
and comes to sing under
your windows.

Goodbye, Winnipeg, goodbye.

MYSTERIES

It is wonderful
what some people
store up and pour out
in old age,
poems and all kinds
of stories,
what journeys they plan,
what voyages
they set their hearts on.

Before starting out
on their travels
they move into new
apartments, settle
on blue tiles
for their bathrooms
and self-cleaning ovens
for their kitchens,
and for their bodies
they decide on a spa
in a country slightly
to the south of them.

How truly one can say
of such people
that they have gained
wisdom; myself I was
spendthrift and stored
neither money nor wisdom,
and I made no plans
to voyage out to far countries,
since all that needs to be seen
can be seen right here
in my own city:

Men with closed faces
selling subway tickets,
science centres,
children packed into
yellow buses, and sealed trucks
loaded with deadly landfill.
in short, a future
full of aging colonels
and empty libraries.

Also rows
of silent schoolgirls
rolling by in wheelchairs,
(of course there is
commerce too people
laughing and talking
and even a cherry tree
that flowers in the spring).

I regret nothing,
I understand nothing;
sometimes it does no harm
to let mysteries remain
mysteries,
no more and no less
confusing
than what we imagine
is ordinary reality.

THE VISITOR

One day
you realize she
may come any time now,
your friend
Ms. Death.

You are
digging dandelions
in the front lawn
you look up
and there she is
smiling and standing
against the cedar hedge,
she's dressed in leaves
loose and flowing
as water and her face
is vague absent and
familiar.

She's new and modern
though she lives
in books and sometimes
steps out of legends,
if you look closely
you'll see
she looks like you
only younger, more silent
and secretive, even
a little mysterious.

You dread her visit
even though you know her,
have dreamed about her,

and for years now
you have traced her every
move in the lines
of your own hand, often
you've heard her skirts
rustle in the next room
the silk of their folds
papery and dry as your own
old lady's skin.

She's very like you,
that motherly apparition,
as she holds out your own
arms to you as she smiles
your own smile at you,
a smile of doubt and
wonderment as she beckons
and calls to you.

And the worst of it is
you know you will answer her,
and in the next instant
you will be gone—
she will wrap you in her shawl
with the cedar fringes,
the one you were knitting
when she came to visit
last summer.

THE ARCHIVIST

1

Her life burst
from its chrysalis
a butterfly;
her body limpid
and luminous
had no wings.

Hummingbirds came,
they dived, hung,
stared, then drank
from neighbouring
milkweed, paused,
thanked her and
flew away.

Then someone,
a magpie or bluejay,
maybe an owl,
set her to turning
words around;
soon she could read
commas and periods,
decipher question marks
and sort through
a thousand layers of
delicate documents.

Sometimes old papers
crumbled in her insect
hands but not before
she had decoded their
molecular messages;

with just her compound eyes
and scanning antennae,
she could push all
the pieces together
so they made sense.

2

She was dutiful;
day and night she
crawled among papers,
her segmented legs
had no memory her
body bore no imprint
of ancestral flight,
or the airy dance
of wings.

Yet occasionally
when she looked up
she could see above her
certain marvels; almost,
she imagined, even
miracles.

In summer
the dust whorls
on roads dizzied her,
and the faraway sound
of snow melting on
mountain-tops always
cooled her.

In autumn
people in red sweaters
raking leaves on the

lawns consoled her,
and in winter when
she slept she heard
the wind rattling
the bare hedges.

3

She longed
to make a journey,
to travel through the
stillness of winter
to find spring, a pot
of gold, and a mother
who loved her.

But the papers
would stretch out
their arms to her
and call after her,
so she would always
put aside miracles
and postpone the world
for later.

Always she postponed
everything for later
after all the myth
of her birth and the
placenta of her destiny
had foretold she would
never fly but as a reward
she could live longer
than the others, much
longer, and she could be
their archivist, she

could record the dreams
of all winged creatures.

Nearly always
the butterflies dreamed
the same things, the smell
of sweetpea liquor the
taste of nasturtium trumpets,
or a tweak from the thumb of
sunlight; occasionally
a rosy clover would pour
a ray of petals into
her eyes and once in a while
a cabbage would fan out
its leaves to cradle her.

4

She recorded it all,
the nectar and the cabbages,
the slim pickings and the
fat plenitudes; she called it
a collage a paste-up of
the world and gave it
a permanent press with drywrap.

So she was surprised
when she saw her collage
had the double shape
of butterfly wings,
that it was a helix
outlined with the cold
fusion of absence, that it
had an aura, that it glowed
in the dark.

The helix burned
with unrelenting furious
power; she recorded
its double spiral and
the way it multiplied and
multiplied and never
stopped multiplying.

Then she recorded
how it killed people.

PEACE NOTES

A leaf, a flower, a child,
September grapes,
red and white carnations
in the rain;
windborn messages
from a distant coastal
city.